CHILDREN'S STORY BOOK COLOUR

MR VIVEK KUMAR PANDEY SHAMBHUNATH

ISBN 979-888546332-4

During writing this book no character & no religious are harmed written by Mr Vivek Kumar Pandey.In This Book 30+ Kid's Story With Moral .This book fully colour edition books. Read & Enjoy.Have A Wonderfull Day.

Contents

Contents

Foreword

Author biography in English :MY NAME IS VIVEK KUMAR PANDEY . I WAS BORN IN 30 SEP 2002,I AM FROM SURAT GUJARAT INDIA.MY DREAM WAS TO BE GOOD WRITERS ,MY FAMILY SUPPORTED ME TO SUCCESSFUL AND I CAN DO IT MY SELF.How do I write? That is a question, I believe, that cannot be honestly answered by me."CELEBRATING YOUNGEST WRITER AWARD WINNER IN GUJARAT 1ST RANK" MR PANDEY JI . I may think I did a good job writing something when in reality it could be horrible. The reader is the one who decides the quality of my writing. I do not find writing to be natural to me and therefore find it to be a real challenge. My trick as a challenged writer is to do the best I can and know that I am happy with the final outcome. It may take a while to do my best and there may be quite a few problems I run into along the way.

I am not a greedy person those who are thinking about me and my self I never tried it anyone people suffering from sadness ,I trying to get promoted people suffering from happiness and joy in your Life Time. Now in current situation in India and also world people are unemployed and have no many but our indian governor help to people to get free food from ration card , i also take part in leadership team ,i am Motivational speaker , Film script writer. There was my two dream firstly writer and secondly actor & also my own film is upcoming soon i done almost completely completed script for my film .I AM GOING TO SAY WORD OF HEART TOUCH OUT PLEASE READ IT" , firstly i thanks my father he supports me in this field they always getting inspired me by own his words and behavior ,they always said that he was a biggest person in the world in future and also they purchase fruit and chocolate for me in anytime & anyway , firstly my father buy him then call me Vivek you want a chocolate i will say yes papa but how many tell me ,papa: you tell me how much i buy him i told 1 or 2 chocolate but my father purchase whole the boxes of chocolate and they get suprised me. MY FATHER WAS BORN IN " 20 SEPTEMBER" 1971 IN INDIA.

1) MY FATHER FAVORITE CLOTHES IS KURTA PAIJMA AND ALSO STYLES SHOE

2) FAVORITE SINGER IS KISHORE DA

3) FAVORITE STATE GUJARAT AND KOLKATA , HIS VILLAGE IN BIHAR

4) FAVORITE COLOR BLACK AND WHITE

THEY ALSO LOVE cricket like IPL and one day t-20 .they also like watching a News daily and heard the song daily ,they also interested in tik tok video but in current time tik tok is banned in india but also few videos are in you tube. In lockdown time my family and me very enjoy day daily. my father play daily ludo with his sister and son, daughter.they always loved tea and coffee anytime call me "। वविके थोडा़ चाय बनाओना वविके तमुहारे हाथ का चाय अच्छा लगता है". I make it tea for my father but some reason after the April to june they are suffering from fever and cough , weakness on 6 June 2020 my father death. they not told me say bye bye his life. After death of 6 June on 10 june my mom and dad anniversary.but my father is Best in the world they can do anything for me please take care of father and respect it of your parents.

1. The Lion and the Mouse

- The Lion and the Mouse

A lion was once sleeping in the jungle when a mouse started running up and down his body just for fun. This disturbed the lion's sleep, and he woke up quite angry. He was about to eat the mouse when the mouse desperately requested the lion to set him free. "I promise you, I will be of great help to you someday if you save me." The lion laughed at the mouse's confidence and let him go.

One day, a few hunters came into the forest and took the lion with them. They tied him up against a tree. The lion was struggling to get out and started to whimper. Soon, the mouse walked past and noticed the lion in trouble. Quickly, he ran and gnawed on the ropes to set the lion free. Both of them sped off into the jungle.

- Moral of the Story

A small act of kindness can go a long way.

2. Count Wisely

- Count Wisely

One day, king Akbar asked a question in his court that left everyone in the courtroom puzzled. As they all tried to figure out the answer, Birbal walked in and asked what the matter was. They repeated the question to him.
The question was, "How many crows are there in the city?"
Birbal immediately smiled and went up to Akbar. He announced the answer; he said there were twenty-one thousand, five hundred and twenty-three crows in the city. When asked how he knew the answer, Birbal replied, "Ask your men to count the number of crows. If there are more, then the relatives of the crows must be visiting them from nearby cities. If there are fewer, then the crows from our city must be visiting their relatives who live outside the city." Pleased with the answer, Akbar presented Birbal with a ruby and pearl chain.

- Moral of the Story

Having an explanation for your answer is just as important as having an answer.

3. The Boy Who Cried Wolf

- The Boy Who Cried Wolf

In a village, lived a carefree boy with his father. The boy's father told him that he was old enough to watch over the sheep while they graze in the fields. Every day, he had to take the sheep to the grassy fields and watch them as they graze. However, the boy was unhappy and didn't want to take the sheep to the fields. He wanted to run and play, not watch the boring sheep graze in the field. So, he decided to have some fun. He cried, "Wolf! Wolf!" until the entire village came running with stones to chase away the wolf before it could eat any of the sheep. When the villagers saw that there was no wolf, they left muttering under their breath about how the boy had wasted their time. The next day, the boy cried once more, "Wolf! Wolf!" and, again, the villagers rushed there to chase the wolf away.
The boy laughed at the fright he had caused. This time, the villagers left angrily. The third day, as the boy went up the small hill, he suddenly saw a wolf attacking his sheep. He cried as hard as he could, "Wolf! Wolf! Wolf!", but not a single villager came to help him. The villagers thought that he was trying to fool them again and did not come to rescue him or his sheep. The little boy lost many sheep that day, all because of his foolishness.

- Moral of the Story

It is difficult to trust people who lie, so it's important to always be truthful.

4. The Fox and the Stork

- The Fox and the Stork

One day, a selfish fox invited a stork for dinner. Stork was very happy with the invitation – she reached the fox's home on time and knocked at the door with her long beak. The fox took her to the dinner table and served some soup in shallow bowls for both of them. As the bowl was too shallow for the stork, she couldn't have soup at all. But, the fox licked up his soup quickly.
The stork was angry and upset, but she didn't show her anger and behaved politely. To teach a lesson to the fox, she then invited him for dinner the next day. She too served soup, but this time the soup was served in two tall narrow vases. The stork devoured the soup from her vase, but the fox couldn't drink any of it because of his narrow neck. The fox realised his mistake and went home famished.

- Moral of the Story

A selfish act backfires sooner or later!

5. The Golden Touch

- The Golden Touch

Once there lived a greedy man in a small town. He was very rich, and he loved gold and all things fancy. But he loved his daughter more than anything. One day, he chanced upon a fairy. The fairy's hair was caught in a few tree branches. He helped her out, but as his greediness took over, he realised that he had an opportunity to become richer by asking for a wish in return (by helping her out). The fairy granted him a wish. He said, "All that I touch should turn to gold." And his wish was granted by the grateful fairy.

The greedy man rushed home to tell his wife and daughter about his wish, all the while touching stones and pebbles and watching them convert into gold. Once he got home, his daughter rushed to greet him. As soon as he bent down to scoop her up in his arms, she turned into a gold statue. He was devastated and started crying and trying to bring his daughter back to life. He realised his folly and spent the rest of his days searching for the fairy to take away his wish.

- Moral of the Story

Greed will always lead to downfall.

6. The Milkmaid and Her Pail

- The Milkmaid and Her Pail

Patty, a milkmaid milked her cow and had two full pails of fresh, creamy milk. She put both pails of milk on a stick and set off to the market to sell the milk. As she took steps towards the market, her thoughts took steps towards wealth. On her way, she kept thinking about the money she would make from selling the milk. Then she thought about what she would do with that money.

She was talking to herself and said, "Once I get the money, I'll buy a chicken. The chicken will lay eggs and I will get more chickens. They'll all lay eggs, and I will sell them for more money. Then, I'll buy the house on the hill and everyone will envy me." She was very happy that soon she would be very rich. With these happy thoughts, she marched ahead. But suddenly, she tripped and fell. Both the pails of the milk fell and all her dreams were shattered. The milk spilt onto the ground, and all Patty could do was cry. "No more dream," she cried foolishly!

- Moral of the Story

Do not count your chickens before they are hatched.

7. Two Frogs With The Same Problem

- Two Frogs With The Same Problem

Once, a group of frogs was roaming around the forest in search of water. Suddenly, two frogs in the group accidentally fell into a deep pit.
The other frogs worried about their friends in the pit.
Seeing how deep the pit was, they told the two frogs that there was no way they could escape the deep pit and that there was no point in trying.
They continued to constantly discourage them as the two frogs tried to jump out of the pit. But keep falling back.
Soon, one of the two frogs started to believe the other frogs — that they'll never be able to escape the pit and eventually died after giving up.
The other frog keeps trying and eventually jumps so high that he escapes the pit. The other frogs were shocked at this and wondered how he did it.
The difference was that the second frog was deaf and couldn't hear the discouragement of the group. He simply thought they were cheering him on!

- Moral of the story

People's opinion of you will affect you, only if you believe it to be so. It's better to believe in yourself.

8. The Potato, The Egg, And The Coffee Beans

- The Potato, The Egg, And The Coffee Beans

A boy named John was upset. His father found him crying.
When his father asked John why he was crying, he said that he had a lot of problems in his life.
His father simply smiled and asked him to get a potato, an egg, and some coffee beans. He placed them in three bowls.
He then asked John to feel their texture and then fill each bowl with water.
John did as he had been told. His father then boiled all three bowls.
Once the bowls had cooled down, John's father asked him to feel the texture of the different food items again.
John noticed that the potato had become soft and its skin was peeling off easily; the egg had become harder and tougher; the coffee beans had completely changed and filled the bowl of water with aroma and flavour.

- Moral of the story

Life will always have problems and pressures, like the boiling water in the story.
It's how you respond and react to these problems that counts the most!

9. The Tortoise And The Hare

- The Tortoise And The Hare

This popular story is about a hare (an animal belonging to the rabbit family), which is known to move quickly and a tortoise, which is known to move slower.

The story began when the hare who has won many races proposed a race with the tortoise. The hare simply wanted to prove that he was the best and have the satisfaction of beating him.

The tortoise agreed and the race began.

The hare got a head-start but became overconfident towards the end of the race. His ego made him believe that he could win the race even if he rested for a while.

And so, he took a nap right near the finish line.

Meanwhile, the tortoise walked slowly but extremely determined and dedicated. He did not give up for a second and kept persevering despite the odds not being in his favour.

While the hare was asleep, the tortoise crossed the finish line and won the race!

The best part was that the tortoise did not gloat or put the hare down!

- Moral of the story

Slow and steady wins the race. When you work hard, stay focused, you can achieve anything, even when it seems impossible.

10. The Elephant Circus

- The Elephant Circus

Once upon a time in a circus, five elephants that performed circus tricks. They were kept tied up with weak rope that they could've easily escaped, but did not. One day, a man visiting the circus asked the ringmaster: "Why haven't these elephants broken the rope and run away?"
The ringmaster replied: "From when they were young, the elephants were made to believe that they were not strong enough to break the ropes and escape."
It was because of this belief that they did not even try to break the ropes now.

- Moral of the story

Don't give in to the limitations of society. Believe that you can achieve everything you want to!

11. The Three Little Pigs

- The Three Little Pigs

Once, there lived three little pigs who were sent out into the world by their mother.
Each of the three little pigs decided to build a house of their own.
The first pig barely put in any effort and built a house made of straw.
The second pig put in a little effort and built a house made of sticks.
The third pig put in a lot of hard work and effort to build a house made of brick and stone.
One fine day, a big bad wolf came to attack each of the three little pigs.
He huffed and puffed and blew away the houses of the first two little pigs that were made of straw and sticks.
He then huffed and puffed but could not blow away the house of the third little pig, who sat snuggly in his house.
Soon, the big bad wolf was breath and ran away.

- Moral of the story

Hard work always pays off. Always think of the bigger picture and don't be lazy.

12. The Monkey And The Crocodile

- The Monkey And The Crocodile

This famous moral story is from the Panchatantra.

There was a monkey that lived on a berry tree on the riverbank. He ate the delicious berries every day.

Once, he saw a crocodile rest under the tree who looked tired and hungry. He gave the crocodile some berries.

The crocodile thanked the monkey. Soon, they became best friends. The monkey gave the crocodile berries every day.

One day, the monkey gave the crocodile extra berries to take home to his wife.

His wife, a wicked crocodile, enjoyed the sweet berries, but then told her husband that she wanted to eat the monkey's heart as that would be sweeter!

The crocodile was upset at first but decided to give in to his wife's wishes.

The next day, he told the monkey that his wife invited the monkey home for dinner.

As the crocodile carried the monkey on his back across the river, he told him about his wife's plan to eat his heart.

The monkey, being smart, told the crocodile that he left his heart on the berry tree and needed to get it.

The crocodile foolishly took him back to the berry tree. On reaching, the monkey climbed onto the tree.

"Who will keep the heart on a tree? You have betrayed my trust. We can never be friends again!" the monkey told his friend.

Sad after losing his friend, the crocodile swims back to his wicked wife.

- Moral of the story

Choose your friends and the people you trust wisely. Moreover, never betray the trust of someone who trusts you.

13. The Elephants And The Mice

- The Elephants And The Mice

Yet another moral story from the Panchatantra.
In an earthquake-hit village abandoned by humans, a colony of mice lived. Near the village was a lake, which was used by a herd of elephants.
The elephants would have to cross the village to go to the lake. Thus, one day, as they walked through, they trampled a lot of mice.

The leader of the mice met with the elephants and requested them to take a different route to the lake. He promised them that they favour would be returned in the time of their need.
The elephants laughed. How could such small mice help these large elephants in any way? But then, they agreed to take a different route.

Not-so-long-after, the mice heard that hunters had caught the herd of elephants and were tied in nets.
Immediately, they rush to rescue the elephants. They gnawed through the nets and ropes with their sharp teeth.
The leader of the elephants repeatedly thanked the mice for their help!

- Moral of the story

A friend in need is a friend indeed. Make sure you help your friends out whenever they need it. They should always be able to count on you.

14. The Foolish Thief

- The Foolish Thief

Once, a wealthy merchant came to King Akbar's court to seek help from Birbal. He suspected that one of his servants had robbed from him.
On hearing this, Birbal thought of a clever plan and summoned the merchant's servants.
He gave each servant a stick of the same length. He told them that the thief's stick would grow two inches by the next day.
The next day, Birbal summoned the servants again. He noticed that a servant's stick was two inches shorter than the others'.
He knew who the thief was.
The foolish thief had cut the stick shorter by two inches as he thought it would grow two inches. Thus, proving his guilt.

- Moral of the story

Truth and justice will always prevail.

15. When Adversity Knocks

- When Adversity Knocks

This is a story that explains how adversity is met differently by different people. There was a girl named Asha who lived with her mother and father in a village. One day, her father assigned her a simple task. He took three vessels filled with boiling water. He placed an egg in one vessel, a potato in the second vessel, and some tea leaves in the third vessel. He asked Asha to keep an eye on the vessels for about ten to fifteen minutes while the three ingredients in three separate vessels boiled. After the said time, he asked Asha to peel the potato and egg, and strain the tea leaves. Asha was left puzzled – she understood her father was trying to explain her something, but she didn't know what it was.

Her father explained, "All three items were put in the same circumstances. See how they've responded differently." He said that the potato turned soft, the egg turned hard, and the tea leaves changed the colour and taste of the water. He further said, "We are all like one of these items. When adversity calls, we respond exactly the way they do. Now, are you a potato, an egg, or tea leaves?"

- Moral of the Story

We can choose how to respond to a difficult situation.

16. The Proud Rose

- The Proud Rose

Once upon a time, there was a beautiful rose plant in a garden. One rose flower on the plant was proud of its beauty. However, it was disappointed that it was growing next to an ugly cactus. Every day, the rose would insult the cactus about its looks, but the cactus stayed quiet. All the other plants in the garden tried to stop the rose from bullying the cactus, but the rose was too swayed by its own beauty to listen to anyone.

One summer, a well in the garden dried up and there was no water for the plants. The rose slowly began to wilt. The rose saw a sparrow dip its beak into the cactus for some water. The rose then felt ashamed for having made fun of the cactus all this time. But because it was in need of water, it went to ask the cactus if it could have some water. The kind cactus agreed, and they both got through summer as friends.

- Moral of the Story

Never judge someone by the way they look.

17. The Tale of the Pencil

- The Tale of the Pencil

A boy named Raj was upset because he had done poorly in his English test. He was sitting in his room when his grandmother came and comforted him. His grandmother sat beside him and gave him a pencil. Raj looked at his grandma puzzled, and said he didn't deserve a pencil after his performance in the test. His grandma explained, "You can learn many things from this pencil because it is just like you. It experiences a painful sharpening, just the way you have experienced the pain of not doing well on your test. However, it will help you be a better student. Just as all the good that comes from the pencil is from within itself, you will also find the strength to overcome this hurdle. And finally, just as this pencil will make its mark on any surface, you too shall leave your mark on anything you choose to." Raj was immediately consoled and promised himself that he would do better.

- Moral of the Story

We all have the strength to be who we wish to be.

18. The Crystal Ball

- The Crystal Ball

Nasir, a small boy, found a crystal ball behind the banyan tree of his garden. The tree told him that it would grant him a wish. He was very happy and he thought hard, but unfortunately, he could not come up with anything he wanted. So, he kept the crystal ball in his bag and waited until he could decide on his wish.

Days went by without him making a wish but his best friend saw him looking at the crystal ball. He stole it from Nasir and showed it to everyone in the village. They all asked for palaces and riches and lots of gold, but could not make more than one wish. In the end, everyone was angry because no one could have everything they wanted. They became very unhappy and decided to ask Nasir for help. Nasir wished that everything would go back to how it was once – before the villagers had tried to satisfy their greed. The palaces and gold vanished and the villagers once again became happy and content.

- Moral of the Story

Money and wealth do not always bring happiness.

19. A Bundle of Sticks

- A Bundle of Sticks

Once upon a time, three neighbours living in a village were having trouble with their crops. Each of the neighbours had one field, but the crops on their fields were infested with pests and were wilting. Every day, they would come up with different ideas to help their crops. The first one tried using a scarecrow in his field, the second used pesticides, and the third built a fence on his field, all to no avail.

One day, the village head came by and called the three farmers. He gave them each a stick and asked them to break it. The farmers could break them easily. He then gave them a bundle of three sticks, and again, asked them to break it. This time, the farmers struggled to break the sticks. The village head said, "Together, you are stronger and work better than you do it alone." The farmers understood what the village head was saying. They pooled in their resources and got rid of the pests from their fields.

- Moral of the Story

There is strength in unity.

20. The Ant and the Dove

- The Ant and the Dove

On a hot scorching day of summer, an ant was walking around in search of water. After walking around for some time, she saw a river and was delighted to see it. She climbed up on a small rock to drink the water, but she slipped and fell into the river. She was drowning but a dove who was sitting on a nearby tree helped her. Seeing the ant in trouble, the dove quickly dropped a leaf into the water. The ant moved towards the leaf and climbed up on it. The dove then carefully pulled the leaf out and placed it on the land. This way, the ant's life was saved and she was forever indebted to the dove.
The ant and the dove became the best of friends and days passed happily. However, one day, a hunter arrived at the forest. He saw the beautiful dove sitting on the tree and aimed his gun at the dove. The ant, who was saved the dove saw this and bit on the heel of the hunter. He shouted from the pain and dropped the gun. The dove was alarmed by the voice of the hunter and realised what could have happened with him. He flew away!

- Moral of the Story

A good deed never goes unrewarded.

21. The Fox and the Grapes

- The Fox and the Grapes

On a hot summer day, a fox wandered across the jungle in order to get some food. He was very hungry and desperately in search of food. He searched everywhere, but couldn't find anything that he could eat. His stomach was rumbling and his search continued. Soon he reached a vineyard which was laden with juicy grapes. The fox looked around to check if he was safe from the hunters. No one was around, so he decided to steal some grapes. He jumped high and high, but he couldn't reach the grapes. The grapes were too high but he refused to give up. The fox jumped high in the air to catch the grapes in his mouth, but he missed. He tried once more but missed again. He tried a few more times, but couldn't reach. It was getting dark and the fox was getting angry. His legs hurt, so he gave up in the end. Walking away, he said, "I'm sure the grapes were sour anyway."

- Moral of the Story

We pretend to hate something when we can't have it.

22. The Ant and the Grasshopper

- The Ant and the Grasshopper

Once upon a time, there were two best friends – an ant and a grasshopper. The grasshopper liked to relax the whole day and play his guitar. The ant, however, would work hard all day. He would collect food from all corners of the garden, while the grasshopper relaxed, played his guitar, or slept. The grasshopper would tell the ant to take a break every day, but the ant would refuse and continue his work. Soon, winter came; days and nights became cold and very few creatures went out.

On a cold day of winter, a colony of ants was busy drying out some grains of corn. The half-dead grasshopper, cold and hungry, came up to the ant who was his friend and asked for a piece of corn. The ant replied, "We work day and night to collect and save up the corn so that we don't die hungry on cold winter days. Why should we give it to you?" The ant further asked, "What were you doing last summer? You should have collected and stored some food. I told you as much before."

The grasshopper said, "I was far too busying singing and sleeping."

The ant replied, "You can sing all winter as far as I am concerned. You will not get anything from us." The ant had enough food to last through the winter, without any worries at all, but the grasshopper didn't and he realised his mistake.

- Moral of the Story

Make hay while the sun shines.

23. The Bear and Two Friends

- The Bear and Two Friends

One day, two best friends were walking on a lonely and dangerous path through a jungle. As the sun began to set, they grew afraid but held on to each other. Suddenly, they saw a bear in their path. One of the boys ran to the nearest tree and climbed it in a jiffy. The other boy did not know how to climb the tree by himself, so he lay on the ground, pretending to be dead. The bear approached the boy on the ground and sniffed around his head. After appearing to whisper something in the boy's ear, the bear went on its way. The boy on the tree climbed down and asked his friend what the bear had whispered in his ear. He replied, "Do not trust friends who do not care for you."

- Moral of the Story

A friend in need is a friend indeed.

24. Friends Forever

- Friends Forever

Once upon a time, there lived a mouse and a frog, who were the best of friends. Every morning, the frog would hop out of the pond to visit the mouse, who lived inside the hole of the tree. He would spend time with the mouse and go back home. One day, the frog realised that he was making too much of an effort to visit the mouse while the mouse never came to meet him at the pond. This made him angry, and he decided to make things right by forcefully taking him to his house.

When the mouse wasn't looking, the frog tied a string to the mouse's tail and tied the other end to his own leg, and hopped away. The mouse started getting dragged with him. Then, the frog jumped into the pond to swim. However, when he looked back, he saw that the mouse had started to drown and was struggling to breathe! The frog quickly untied the string from his tail and took him to the shore. Seeing the mouse with his eyes barely open made the frog very sad, and he immediately regretted pulling him into the pond.

- Moral of the Story

Don't take revenge because it can be harmful to you.

25. The Elephant and Her Friends

- The Elephant and Her Friends

Once upon a time, a lone elephant made her way into a strange forest. It was new to her, and she was looking to make friends. She approached a monkey and said, "Hello, monkey! Would you like to be my friend?" The monkey said, "You are too big to swing like me, so I can't be your friend." The elephant then went to a rabbit and asked the same question. The rabbit said, "You are too big to fit in my burrow, so I can't be your friend." The elephant also went to the frog in the pond and asked the same question. The frog replied, "You are too heavy to jump as high as me, so I can't be your friend."

The elephant was really sad because she couldn't make friends. Then, one day, she saw all the animals running deeper into the forest, and she asked a bear what the fuss was about. The bear said, "The lion is on the loose – they are running from him to save themselves." The elephant went up to the lion and said, "Please don't hurt these innocent people. Please leave them alone." The lion scoffed and asked the elephant to move aside. Then, the elephant got angry and pushed the lion with all her might, injuring him. All the other animals came out slowly and started to rejoice about the lion's defeat. They went to the elephant and said to her, "You are just the right size to be our friend!"

- Moral of the Story

A person's size does not determine their worth.

26. The Woodcutter and the Golden Axe

- The Woodcutter and the Golden Axe

There was once a woodcutter, working hard in the forest, getting wood to sell for some food. As he was cutting a tree, his axe accidentally fell into the river. The river was deep and was flowing really fast – he lost his axe and could not find it again. He sat at the bank of the river and wept.

While he wept, the God of the river arose and asked him what happened. The woodcutter told him the story. The God of the river offered to help him by looking for his axe. He disappeared into the river and retrieved a golden axe, but the woodcutter said it was not his. He disappeared again and came back with a silver axe, but the woodcutter said that was not his either. The God disappeared into the water again and came back with an iron axe – the woodcutter smiled and said it was his. The God was impressed with the woodcutter's honesty and gifted him both the golden and silver axes.

- Moral of the Story

Honesty is the best policy.

27. The Needle Tree

- The Needle Tree

There lived two brothers near a forest. The elder one was very mean to the younger brother – he would finish all the food and wear all the new clothes of his younger brother. One day, the elder brother decided to go into the forest to get some firewood and sell it in the market. As he went around, chopping tree after tree, he stumbled upon a magical tree. The tree said, "Oh kind sir, please do not cut my branches. If you spare me, I will give you golden apples." He agreed, but was left disappointed with the number of apples the tree gave him. As greed overcame him, he threatened the tree that he will cut the entire trunk if it didn't give him more apples. The magical tree, instead, showered upon the elder brother, hundreds and hundreds of tiny needles. The elder brother lay on the ground, crying in pain, as the sun set.

The younger brother was worried and so he went in search of his elder brother. He found him lying in pain near the tree, with hundreds of needles on his body. He rushed to his brother and removed each needle, lovingly and gently. After he finished, the elder brother apologised for treating him badly and promised to be better. The tree saw the change in the elder brother's heart and gave them all the golden apples they would ever need.

- Moral of the Story

It is important to be kind and gracious, as it will always be rewarded.

28. The Greedy Lion

- The Greedy Lion

On a hot day, a lion in the forest started feeling hungry. He was starting to hunt for his food when he found a hare roaming around alone. Instead of catching the hare, the lion let it go – "A small hare such as this can't satisfy my hunger", he said and scoffed. Then, a beautiful deer passed by and he decided to take his chances – he ran and ran behind the deer but since he was weak because of the hunger, he struggled to keep up with the deer's speed. Tired and defeated, the lion went back to look for the hare to fill up his stomach for the time being, but it was gone. The lion was sad and remained hungry for a long time.

- Moral of the Story

Greed is never a good thing.

29. The Tale of Peter Rabbit

- The Tale of Peter Rabbit

ONCE upon a time there were four little Rabbits, and their names were—Flopsy, Mopsy, Cotton-tail, and Peter.

They lived with their Mother in a sand-bank, underneath the root of a very big fir tree.

"NOW, my dears," said old Mrs. Rabbit one morning, "you may go into the fields or down the lane, but don't go into Mr. McGregor's garden: your Father had an accident there; he was put in a pie by Mrs. McGregor."

"NOW run along, and don't get into mischief. I am going out."

THEN old Mrs. Rabbit took a basket and her umbrella, to the baker's. She bought a loaf of brown bread and five currant buns.

FLOPSY, Mopsy, and Cottontail, who were good little bunnies, went down the lane to gather blackberries;

BUT Peter, who was very naughty, ran straight away to Mr. McGregor's garden and squeezed under the gate!

FIRST he ate some lettuces and some French beans; and then he ate some radishes;

AND then, feeling rather sick, he went to look for some parsley.

BUT round the end of a cucumber frame, whom should he meet but Mr. McGregor!

MR. McGREGOR was on his hands and knees planting out young cabbages, but he jumped up and ran after Peter, waving a rake and calling out, "Stop thief!"

PETER was most dreadfully frightened; he rushed all over the garden, for he had forgotten the way back to the gate.

He lost one of his shoes among the cabbages, and the other shoe amongst the potatoes.

AFTER losing them, he ran on four legs and went faster, so that I think he might have got away altogether if he had not unfortunately run into a gooseberry net, and got caught by the large buttons on his jacket. It was a blue jacket with brass buttons, quite new.

PETER gave himself up for lost, and shed big tears; but his sobs were overheard by some friendly sparrows, who flew to him in great excitement, and implored him to exert himself.

MR. McGREGOR came up with a sieve, which he intended to pop upon the top of Peter; but Peter wriggled out just in time, leaving his jacket behind him.

AND rushed into the toolshed, and jumped into a can. It would have been a beautiful thing to hide in, if it had not had so much water in it.

MR. McGREGOR was quite sure that Peter was somewhere in the toolshed, perhaps hidden underneath a flower-pot. He began to turn them over carefully, looking under each.

Presently Peter sneezed— "Kertyschoo!" Mr. McGregor was after him in no time,

AND tried to put his foot upon Peter, who jumped out of a window, upsetting three plants. The window was too small for Mr. McGregor, and he was tired of running after Peter. He went back to his work.

PETER sat down to rest; he was out of breath and trembling with fright, and he had not the least idea which way to go. Also he was very damp with sitting in that can.

After a time he began to wander about, going lippity— lippity—not very fast, and looking all around.

HE found a door in a wall; but it was locked, and there was no room for a fat little rabbit to squeeze underneath.

An old mouse was running in and out over the stone doorstep, carrying peas and beans to her family in the wood. Peter asked her the way to the gate, but she had such a large pea in her mouth that she could not answer. She only shook her head at him. Peter began to cry.

THEN he tried to find his way straight across the garden, but he became more and more puzzled. Presently, he came to a pond where Mr. McGregor filled his water-cans. A white cat was staring at some gold-fish; she sat very, very still, but now and then the tip of her tail twitched as if it were alive. Peter thought it best to go away without speaking to her; he had heard about cats from his cousin, little Benjamin Bunny.

HE went back towards the tool-shed, but suddenly, quite close to him, he heard the noise of a hoe—scr-r-ritch, scratch, scratch, scritch. Peter scuttered underneath the bushes. But presently, as nothing happened, he came out, and climbed upon a wheelbarrow, and peeped over. The first thing he saw was Mr. McGregor hoeing onions. His back was turned towards Peter, and beyond him was the gate!

PETER got down very quietly off the wheelbarrow, and started running as fast as he could go, along a straight walk behind some black-currant bushes.

Mr. McGregor caught sight of him at the corner, but Peter did not care. He slipped underneath the gate, and was safe at last in the wood outside the garden.

MR. McGREGOR hung up the little jacket and the shoes for a scare-crow to frighten the blackbirds.

PETER never stopped running or looked behind him till he got home to the big fir-tree.

He was so tired that he flopped down upon the nice soft sand on the floor of the rabbit-hole, and shut his eyes. His mother was busy cooking; she wondered what he had done with his clothes. It was the second little jacket and pair of shoes that Peter had lost in a fortnight!

I AM sorry to say that Peter was not very well during the evening.

His mother put him to bed, and made some camomile tea; and she gave a dose of it to Peter!

"One table-spoonful to be taken at bed-time."

BUT Flopsy, Mopsy, and Cotton-tail had bread and milk and blackberries, for supper.

THE END

30. The Elves and The Shoemaker

- The Elves and The Shoemaker

FIRST STORY

A shoemaker, by no fault of his own, had become so poor that at last he had nothing left but leather for one pair of shoes. So in the evening, he cut out the shoes which he wished to begin to make the next morning, and as he had a good conscience, he lay down quietly in his bed, commended himself to God, and fell asleep. In the morning, after he had said his prayers, and was just going to sit down to work, the two shoes stood quite finished on his table. He was astounded, and knew not what to say to it. He took the shoes in his hands to observe them closer, and they were so neatly made that there was not one bad stitch in them, just as if they were intended as a masterpiece. Soon after, a buyer came in, and as the shoes pleased him so well, he paid more for them than was customary, and, with the money, the shoemaker was able to purchase leather for two pairs of shoes. He cut them out at night, and next morning was about to set to work with fresh courage; but he had no need to do so, for, when he got up, they were already made, and buyers also were not wanting, who gave him money enough to buy leather for four pairs of shoes. The following morning, too, he found the four pairs made; and so it went on constantly, what he cut out in the evening was finished by the morning, so that he soon had his honest independence again, and at last became a wealthy man. Now it befell that one evening not long before Christmas, when the man had been cutting out, he said to his wife, before going to bed, "What think you if we were to stay up to-night to see who it is that lends us this helping hand?" The woman liked the idea, and lighted a candle, and then they hid themselves in a corner of the room, behind some clothes which were hanging up there, and watched. When

it was midnight, two pretty little naked men came, sat down by the shoemaker's table, took all the work which was cut out before them and began to stitch, and sew, and hammer so skilfully and so quickly with their little fingers that the shoemaker could not turn away his eyes for astonishment. They did not stop until all was done, and stood finished on the table, and they ran quickly away. Next morning the woman said, "The little men have made us rich, and we really must show that we are grateful for it. They run about so, and have nothing on, and must be cold. I'll tell thee what I'll do: I will make them little shirts, and coats, and vests, and trousers, and knit both of them a pair of stockings, and do thou, too, make them two little pairs of shoes." The man said, "I shall be very glad to do it;" and one night, when everything was ready, they laid their presents all together on the table instead of the cut-out work, and then concealed themselves to see how the little men would behave. At midnight they came bounding in, and wanted to get to work at once, but as they did not find any leather cut out, but only the pretty little articles of clothing, they were at first astonished, and then they showed intense delight. They dressed themselves with the greatest rapidity, putting the pretty clothes on, and singing,
"Now we are boys so fine to see,
Why should we longer cobblers be?"
Then they danced and skipped and leapt over chairs and benches. At last they danced out of doors. From that time forth they came no more, but as long as the shoemaker lived all went well with him, and all his undertakings prospered.

- SECOND STORY

There was once a poor servant-girl, who was industrious and cleanly, and swept the house every day, and emptied her sweepings on the great heap in front of the door. One morning when she was just going back to her work, she found a letter on this heap, and as she could not read, she put her broom in the corner, and took the letter to her master and mistress, and behold it was an invitation from the elves, who asked the girl to hold a child for them at its christening.

The girl did not know what to do, but at length, after much persuasion, and as they told her that it was not right to refuse an invitation of this kind, she consented. Then three elves came and conducted her to a hollow mountain, where the little folks lived. Everything there was small, but more elegant and beautiful than can be described. The baby's mother lay in a bed of black ebony ornamented with pearls, the coverlids were embroidered with gold, the cradle was of ivory, the bath of gold. The girl stood as godmother, and then wanted to go home again, but the little elves urgently entreated her to stay three days with them. So she stayed, and passed the time in pleasure and gaiety, and the little folks did all they could to make her happy. At last she set out on her way home. Then first they filled her pockets quite full of money, and after that they led her out of the mountain again. When she got home, she wanted to begin her work, and took the broom, which was still standing in the corner, in her hand and began to sweep. Then some strangers came out of the house, who asked her who she was, and what business she had there? And she had not, as she thought, been three days with the little men in the mountains, but seven years, and in the meantime her former masters had died.

- THIRD STORY

A certain mother's child had been taken away out of its cradle by the elves, and a changeling with a large head and staring eyes, which would do nothing but eat and drink, laid in its place. In her trouble she went to her neighbour, and asked her advice. The neighbour said that she was to carry the changeling into the kitchen, set it down on the hearth, light a fire, and boil some water in two egg-shells, which would make the changeling laugh, and if he laughed, all would be over with him. The woman did everything that her neighbour bade her. When she put the egg-shells with water on the fire, the imp said, "I am as old now as the Wester forest, but never yet have I seen any one boil anything in an egg-shell!" And he began to laugh at it. Whilst he was laughing, suddenly came a host of little elves, who brought the right child, set it down on the hearth, and took the changeling away with them.

31. The Bogey-Beast

- The Bogey-Beast

There was once a woman who was very, very cheerful, though she had little to make her so; for she was old, and poor, and lonely. She lived in a little bit of a cottage and earned a scant living by running errands for her neighbours, getting a bite here, a sup there, as reward for her services. So she made shift to get on, and always looked as spry and cheery as if she had not a want in the world.

Now one summer evening, as she was trotting, full of smiles as ever, along the high road to her hovel, what should she see but a big black pot lying in the ditch!

"Goodness me!" she cried, "that would be just the very thing for me if I only had something to put in it! But I haven't! Now who could have left it in the ditch?"

And she looked about her expecting the owner would not be far off; but she could see nobody.

"Maybe there is a hole in it," she went on, "and that's why it has been cast away. But it would do fine to put a flower in for my window; so I'll just take it home with me."

And with that she lifted the lid and looked inside. "Mercy me!" she cried, fair amazed. "If it isn't full of gold pieces. Here's luck!"

And so it was, brimful of great gold coins. Well, at first she simply stood stock-still, wondering if she was standing on her head or her heels. Then she began saying:

"Lawks! But I do feel rich. I feel awful rich!"

After she had said this many times, she began to wonder how she was to get her treasure home. It was too heavy for her to carry, and she could see no better way than to tie the end of her shawl to it and drag it behind her like a go-cart.

"It will soon be dark," she said to herself as she trotted along. "So much the better! The neighbours will not see what I'm bringing home, and I shall have all the night to myself, and be able to think what I'll do! Mayhap I'll buy a grand house and just sit by the fire with a cup o' tea and do no work at all like a queen. Or maybe I'll bury it at the garden foot and just keep a bit in the old china teapot on the chimney-piece. Or maybe—Goody! Goody! I feel that grand I don't know myself."

By this time she was a bit tired of dragging such a heavy weight, and, stopping to rest a while, turned to look at her treasure.

And lo! it wasn't a pot of gold at all! It was nothing but a lump of silver.

She stared at it, and rubbed her eyes, and stared at it again.

"Well! I never!" she said at last. "And me thinking it was a pot of gold! I must have been dreaming. But this is luck! Silver is far less trouble—easier to mind, and not so easy stolen. Them gold pieces would have been the death o' me, and with this great lump of silver—"

So she went off again planning what she would do, and feeling as rich as rich, until becoming a bit tired again she stopped to rest and gave a look round to see if her treasure was safe; and she saw nothing but a great lump of iron!

"Well! I never!" says she again. "And I mistaking it for silver! I must have been dreaming. But this is luck! It's real convenient. I can get penny pieces for old iron, and penny pieces are a deal handier for me than your gold and silver. Why! I should never have slept a wink for fear of being robbed. But a penny piece comes in useful, and I shall sell that iron for a lot and be real rich—rolling rich."

So on she trotted full of plans as to how she would spend her penny pieces, till once more she stopped to rest and looked round to see her treasure was safe. And this time she saw nothing but a big stone.

"Well! I never!" she cried, full of smiles. "And to think I mistook it for iron. I must have been dreaming. But here's luck indeed, and me wanting a stone terrible bad to stick open the gate. Eh my! but it's a change for the better! It's a fine thing to have good luck."

So, all in a hurry to see how the stone would keep the gate open, she trotted off down the hill till she came to her own cottage. She unlatched the gate and then turned to unfasten her shawl from the stone which lay on the path behind her. Aye! It was a stone sure enough. There was plenty light to see it lying there, douce and peaceable as a stone should.

So she bent over it to unfasten the shawl end, when—"Oh my!" All of a sudden it gave a jump, a squeal, and in one moment was as big as a haystack. Then it let down four great lanky legs and threw out two long ears, nourished a great long tail and romped off, kicking and squealing and whinnying and laughing like a naughty, mischievous boy!

The old woman stared after it till it was fairly out of sight, then she burst out laughing too.

"Well!" she chuckled, "I am in luck! Quite the luckiest body hereabouts. Fancy my seeing the Bogey-Beast all to myself; and making myself so free with it too! My goodness! I do feel that uplifted—that GRAND!"—

So she went into her cottage and spent the evening chuckling over her good luck.

32. Little Red Riding Hood

- Little Red Riding Hood

Once upon a time there was a dear little girl who was loved by every one who looked at her, but most of all by her grandmother, and there was nothing that she would not have given to the child. Once she gave her a little cap of red velvet, which suited her so well that she would never wear anything else. So she was always called Little Red Riding Hood.

One day her mother said to her, "Come, Little Red Riding Hood, here is a piece of cake and a bottle of wine. Take them to your grandmother, she is ill and weak, and they will do her good. Set out before it gets hot, and when you are going, walk nicely and quietly and do not run off the path, or you may fall and break the bottle, and then your grandmother will get nothing. And when you go into her room, don't forget to say, good-morning, and don't peep into every corner before you do it."

I will take great care, said Little Red Riding Hood to her mother, and gave her hand on it.

The grandmother lived out in the wood, half a league from the village, and just as Little Red Riding Hood entered the wood, a wolf met her. Little Red Riding Hood did not know what a wicked creature he was, and was not at all afraid of him.

"Good-day, Little Red Riding Hood," said he.

"Thank you kindly, wolf."

"Whither away so early, Little Red Riding Hood?"

"To my grandmother's."

"What have you got in your apron?"

"Cake and wine. Yesterday was baking-day, so poor sick grandmother is to have something good, to make her stronger."

"Where does your grandmother live, Little Red Riding Hood?"

"A good quarter of a league farther on in the wood. Her house stands under the three large oak-trees, the nut-trees are just below. You surely must know it," replied Little Red Riding Hood.

The wolf thought to himself, "What a tender young creature. What a nice plump mouthful, she will be better to eat than the old woman. I must act craftily, so as to catch both." So he walked for a short time by the side of Little Red Riding Hood, and then he said, "see Little Red Riding Hood, how pretty the flowers are about here. Why do you not look round. I believe, too, that you do not hear how sweetly the little birds are singing. You walk gravely along as if you were going to school, while everything else out here in the wood is merry."

Little Red Riding Hood raised her eyes, and when she saw the sunbeams dancing here and there through the trees, and pretty flowers growing everywhere, she thought, suppose I take grandmother a fresh nosegay. That would please her too. It is so early in the day that I shall still get there in good time. And so she ran from the path into the wood to look for flowers. And whenever she had picked one, she fancied that she saw a still prettier one farther on, and ran after it, and so got deeper and deeper into the wood.

Meanwhile the wolf ran straight to the grandmother's house and knocked at the door.

"Who is there?"

"Little Red Riding Hood," replied the wolf. "She is bringing cake and wine. Open the door."

"Lift the latch," called out the grandmother, "I am too weak, and cannot get up."

The wolf lifted the latch, the door sprang open, and without saying a word he went straight to the grandmother's bed, and devoured her. Then he put on her clothes, dressed himself in her cap, laid himself in bed and drew the curtains.

Little Red Riding Hood, however, had been running about picking flowers, and when she had gathered so many that she could carry no more, she remembered her grandmother, and set out on the way to her.

She was surprised to find the cottage-door standing open, and when she went into the room, she had such a strange feeling that she said to herself, oh dear, how uneasy I feel to-day, and at other times I like being with grandmother so much.

She called out, "Good morning," but received no answer. So she went to the bed and drew back the curtains. There lay her grandmother with her cap pulled far over her face, and looking very strange.

"Oh, grandmother," she said, "what big ears you have."

"The better to hear you with, my child," was the reply.

"But, grandmother, what big eyes you have," she said.

"The better to see you with, my dear."

"But, grandmother, what large hands you have."

"The better to hug you with."

"Oh, but, grandmother, what a terrible big mouth you have."

"The better to eat you with."

And scarcely had the wolf said this, than with one bound he was out of bed and swallowed up Little Red Riding Hood.

When the wolf had appeased his appetite, he lay down again in the bed, fell asleep and began to snore very loud. The huntsman was just passing the house, and thought to himself, how the old woman is snoring. I must just see if she wants anything.

So he went into the room, and when he came to the bed, he saw that the wolf was lying in it. "Do I find you here, you old sinner," said he. "I have long sought you."

Then just as he was going to fire at him, it occurred to him that the wolf might have devoured the grandmother, and that she might still be saved, so he did not fire, but took a pair of scissors, and began to cut open the stomach of the sleeping wolf.

When he had made two snips, he saw the Little Red Riding Hood shining, and then he made two snips more, and the little girl sprang out, crying, "Ah, how frightened I have been. How dark it was inside the wolf."

And after that the aged grandmother came out alive also, but scarcely able to breathe. Little Red Riding Hood, however, quickly fetched great stones with which they filled the wolf's belly, and when he awoke, he wanted to run away, but the stones were so heavy that he collapsed at once, and fell dead.

Then all three were delighted. The huntsman drew off the wolf's skin and went home with it. The grandmother ate the cake and drank the wine which Little Red Riding Hood had brought, and revived, but Little Red Riding Hood thought to herself, as long as I live, I will never by myself leave the path, to run into the wood, when my mother has forbidden me to do so.

It is also related that once when Little Red Riding Hood was again taking cakes to the old grandmother, another wolf spoke to her, and tried to entice her from the path. Little Red Riding Hood, however, was on her guard, and went straight forward on her way, and told her grandmother that she had met the wolf, and that he had said good-morning to her, but with such a wicked look in his eyes, that if they had not been on the public road she was certain he would have eaten her up. "Well," said the grandmother, "we will shut the door, that he may not come in."

Soon afterwards the wolf knocked, and cried, "open the door, grandmother, I am Little Red Riding Hood, and am bringing you some cakes."

But they did not speak, or open the door, so the grey-beard stole twice or thrice round the house, and at last jumped on the roof, intending to wait until Little Red Riding Hood went home in the evening, and then to steal after her and devour her in the darkness. But the grandmother saw what was in his thoughts. In front of the house was a great stone trough, so she said to the child, take the pail, Little Red Riding Hood. I made some sausages yesterday, so carry the water in which I boiled them to the trough. Little Red Riding Hood carried until the great trough was quite full. Then the smell of the sausages reached the wolf, and he sniffed and peeped down, and at last stretched out his neck so far that he could no longer keep his footing and began to slip, and slipped down from the roof straight into the great trough, and was drowned. But Little Red Riding Hood went joyously home, and no one ever did anything to harm her again.

33. Snow White

- Snow White

There was once a queen who had no children, and it grieved her sorely. One winter's afternoon she was sitting by the window sewing when she pricked her finger, and three drops of blood fell on the snow. Then she thought to herself:
"Ah, what would I give to have a daughter with skin as white as snow and cheeks as red as blood."
After a while a little daughter came to her with skin as white as snow and cheeks as red as blood. So they called her Snow White.
But before Snow White had grown up, her mother, the Queen, died and her father married again, a most beautiful princess who was very vain of her beauty and jealous of all women who might be thought as beautiful as she was. And every morning she used to stand before her mirror and say:
"Mirror, mirror, on the wall, Who is the fairest of us all?"
And the mirror always used to reply:
"Queen, Queen, on thy throne, The greatest beauty is thine own."
But Snow White grew fairer and fairer every year, till at last one day when the Queen in the morning spoke to her mirror and said:
"Mirror, mirror, on the wall, Who is the fairest of us all?"
the mirror replied:
"Queen, Queen, on thy throne, Snow White's the fairest thou must own."
Then the Queen grew terribly jealous of Snow White and thought and thought how she could get rid of her, till at last she went to a hunter and engaged him for a large sum of money to take Snow White out into the forest and there kill her and bring back her heart.

But when the hunter had taken Snow White out into the forest and thought to kill her, she was so beautiful that his heart failed him, and he let her go, telling her she must not, for his sake and for her own, return to the King's palace. Then he killed a deer and took back the heart to the Queen, telling her that it was the heart of Snow White.

Snow White wandered on and on till she got through the forest and came to a mountain hut and knocked at the door, but she got no reply. She was so tired that she lifted up the latch and walked in, and there she saw three little beds and three little chairs and three little cupboards all ready for use. And she went up to the first bed and lay down upon it, but it was so hard that she couldn't rest; and then she went up to the second bed and lay down upon that, but that was so soft that she got too hot and couldn't go to sleep. So she tried the third bed, but that was neither too hard nor too soft, but suited her exactly; and she fell asleep there.

In the evening the owners of the hut, who were three little dwarfs who earned their living by digging coal in the hills, came back to their home. And when they came in, after they had washed themselves, they went to their beds, and the first of them said:

"Somebody has been sleeping in my bed!"

And then the second one said:

"And somebody's been sleeping in my bed!"

And the third one called out in a shrill voice, for he was so excited:

"Somebody is sleeping in my bed, just look how beautiful she is!"

So they waited till she woke up, and asked her how she had come there, and she told them all that the hunter had said to her about the Queen wanting to slay her.

Then the dwarfs asked her if she would be willing to stop with them and keep house for them; and she said that she would be delighted.

Next morning the Queen went up as usual to her mirror, and called out:

"Mirror, mirror, on the wall, Who is the fairest of us all?"

And the mirror answered as usual:

"Queen, Queen, on thy throne, Snow White's the fairest thou must own."

And the Queen knew that Snow White had not been slain. So she sent for the hunter and made him confess that he had let Snow White go; and she made him search about beyond the forest, till at last he brought back word to her that Snow White was dwelling in a little hut on the hill with some coal-miners.

Then the Queen dressed herself up like an old woman, and, taking a poisoned comb with her, went back the next day to the hut where Snow White was living. Now the dwarfs had warned her not to open the door to anybody lest evil might befall her; and she found it very lonesome keeping always within doors.

When the Queen, disguised as an old woman, came to the door of the house she knocked upon it with her stick, but Snow White called out from within:

"Who is there? Go away! I must not let anybody come in."

"All right," answered the Queen. "If you can come to the window we can have a little chat there, and I can show you my wares."

So when Snow White came to the window the Queen said:

"Oh, what beautiful black hair; you ought to have a comb to bind it up;" and she showed her the comb that she had brought with her.

But Snow White said:

"I have no money and cannot afford to buy so fine a comb."

Then the Queen said:

"That is no matter; perhaps you have something golden that you can give me in exchange."

And Snow White thought of a golden ring that her father had given to her, and offered to give it for the comb. The Queen took it and gave Snow White the comb and bade her good-bye, and went back to the palace.

Snow White lost no time in going to the mirror, and binding up her hair and putting the comb into it. But it had scarcely been in her hair a few minutes when she fell down as if she were dead, and all the blood left her cheeks, and she was Snow White indeed.

When the dwarfs came home that evening they were surprised to find that the table was not spread for them, and looking about they soon found Snow White lying upon the ground as if she were dead. But one of them listened to her heart and said: "She lives! She lives!"

And they began to consider what caused Snow White to fall into such a swoon. They soon found the comb, and when they took it out Snow White soon opened her eyes and became as lively as she ever was before.

Next morning the Queen went to the mirror on the wall and said to it:

"Mirror, mirror, on the wall, Who is the fairest of us all?"

Then the mirror said as before:

"Queen, Queen, on thy throne, Snow White's the fairest thou must own."

Then the Queen knew that something had happened to the comb and that Snow White was still alive. So she dressed herself once more as an old woman and took with her a poisoned ribbon and went to the hut of the three dwarfs. And when she got there she knocked at the door, but Snow White called out:

"You cannot enter; I must not open the door."

Then, as before, the Queen called out in reply:

"Then come to the window, and you can see my wares."

When Snow White came to the window the Queen said:

"You are looking more beautiful than ever, but how unbecomingly you arrange your hair. Did you use that comb I gave you yesterday?"

"Yes, indeed," said Snow White, "and I fell into a swoon because of it; I am afraid there is something the matter with it."

"No, no, that cannot be," said the Queen; "there must be some mistake. But if you cannot use the comb I will let you have this pretty ribbon instead," and she held out the poisoned ribbon. Snow White took it, and after the old woman, as she thought she was, had gone away, Snow White went to the mirror and tied up her hair with the piece of ribbon. But scarcely had she done so when she fell to the ground lifeless and lay there as if she were dead.

That evening the dwarfs came home and found Snow White lying on the ground as if dead, but soon discovered the poisoned ribbon and untied it; and almost as soon as this was done Snow White revived again.

Next morning the Queen went once more to the mirror on the wall, and called out:

"Mirror, mirror, on the wall, Who is the fairest of us all?"

to which the mirror replied, without any change:

"Queen, Queen, on thy throne, Snow White's the fairest thou must own."

And the Queen recognized that once again her plans had failed, and Snow White was still alive. So she dressed herself once more and took with her a poisoned apple, which was so arranged that only one half of it was poisoned and the rest of it was left as before. And when the Queen got to the hut of the dwarfs she tried to open the door, but Snow White called out:

"You can't come in!"

"Then I'll come to the window," said the Queen.

"Ah, you are the old lady that came twice before; you have not brought me good luck, each time something has befallen me."

But the Queen said:

"I do not know how that can be; I only brought you something for your hair; perhaps you tied it too tight. To show you that I have no ill-will against you I have brought you this beautiful apple."

"But my guardians," said Snow White, "told me that I must take nothing more from you."

"Oh, this is nothing to wear," said the Queen, "this is something to eat. To show you that there can be no harm in it I will take half of it myself and you shall eat the other half."

So she cut the apple in two and gave the poisoned half to Snow White. And the moment she had swallowed the first bite of it she fell down dead. Then the Queen slunk away and went back to the palace and went at once to her chamber and addressed the mirror on the wall:

"Mirror, mirror, on the wall, Who is the fairest of us all?"

And this time the mirror answered, as it used to do:

"Queen, Queen, on thy throne, The greatest beauty is thine own."

Then the Queen knew that Snow White was dead at last, and that she was without a rival in beauty.

When the dwarfs came home that night they found Snow White lying upon the ground quite dead, and could not find out what had happened or how they could cure her. But, though she seemed dead, Snow White kept her beautiful white skin and seemed more like a statue than a dead person. So the dwarfs had a glass coffer made, and put Snow White in and locked it up. And she remained there for days and days without changing the slightest, looking oh, so beautiful under the glass case.

Now a great prince of the neighbouring country happened to be hunting near the hill of the dwarfs and called at their hut to get a glass of water. And when he came in he found nobody there but Snow White lying in her crystal coffer. And he fell at once in love with her and sat by her side till the dwarfs came home, and he asked them who she was. Then they told him her history, and he begged that he might carry the coffer away so that he might always have her near him. At first they would not do so. But he showed how much he loved her, so that they at last yielded, and he called for his men to carry the coffer home to his palace.

And when the men commenced carrying the coffer down the mountain they jolted it so much that the piece of poisoned apple in Snow White's throat fell out, and she revived and opened her eyes and looked upon the Prince who was riding by her side. Then he ordered the coffer to be opened, and told her all that had happened. And he took her home to his castle and married her.

After this happened the Queen once more came to her room and spoke to the mirror on the wall and said:

"Mirror, mirror, on the wall, Who is the fairest of us all?"

And the mirror this time said again:

"Queen, Queen, on thy throne, Snow White's the fairest thou must own."

Printed by Libri Plureos GmbH in Hamburg,
Germany